I0060307

IMPLEMENTING INTELLIGENCE–LED POLICING IN NIGERIA

A Concise Guide and Strategy for the Nigeria Police Force

DR CHARLES OMOLE

Copyright 2017

By

Charles Omole

ISBN: 978-1-907095-25-2

Published by:

WINNING FAITH

London . New York . Lagos

TABLE OF CONTENTS

DEDICATION

This book is dedicated to the serving officers of the Nigeria Police Force who are doing a great job despite the challenges they face and a public that do not fully appreciate their courage and difficulties. Keep up the good work all of you as better days are ahead.

INTRODUCTION

This book has been written with the hope and intention that all Nigeria Police Officers will get a copy at some point in their career. As a result, I have used more standard language that can be easily understood by all.

The challenges of literacy and poor educational system that affects the wider Nigerian population also reflect in the police with its varying level of literacy and literary comprehension amongst its officers.

I need to make sure readers will be left in doubt what the principles in this book mean and how they can be deployed. These considerations shaped my approach to this book project.

When I presented my previous almost 400-page book on 'Good Governance in the Nigeria

Police' to serving officers in the Nigeria Police, many complained that it is too big and were discouraged from reading it. So I have deliberately made this book smaller and condensed my thoughts in a way to encourage the widest readership.

Intelligence-led policing is a recent but growing doctrine in policing globally. With the advent of modern technology and growth in its adoption by the citizenry, it is a matter of time before old policing techniques will become obsolete in the face of more astute criminal population, terror and security threats across the globe.

Therefore, adoption and implementation of Intelligence-led policing is a necessity for any police organization in the world who want to be more effective and efficient in an era of declining global budgetary allocation by national governments.

Intelligence-led policing is not widely known or understood by most of the serving officers of the Nigeria police. There are some who are familiar with its concepts through their exposure to United Nations and other International assignments, but these officers are few in number. Consequently, the Nigeria Police Force have institutionally not deployed this policing system operationally, although the seed of it exists in various forms but not in a joined up way.

This book will explain what Intelligence-led policing is, the challenges facing its adoption by the Nigerian police and recommendations on how it can be deployed and adopted across the policing estate in Nigeria.

This book does not pretend to be a detailed study of Intelligence–led policing; but a concise publication aimed to introduce its basic concepts and operational strategies that will allow for a deeper study if needed. The book will also bluntly expose the folly of politicians who have weakened the Nigerian police through proliferation of many policing agencies with overlapping responsibilities. Such multiple and duplicated policing arrangements do not support effective implementation of Intelligence-led policing. Some recommendations are made to address this challenge.

Finally, there will be enough in this book to capture the interest of all serving officers and enable them to buy-in into Intelligence-led policing as stakeholders in the operational excellence of this doctrine in the Nigerian police.

It is a publication designed to be a "pocket book" so to speak that will be referenced by officers after a training exercise on this same topic. That is why I have reproduced key parts of the Police Act at the end of this book to make this a good reference book for serving officers. It is not impossible that I will produced a more detailed textbook on this subject matter in the future.

The future of policing in Nigeria is bright indeed as they are more educated and enlightened than they have ever been. This book is another contribution to supporting the police and developing capacity in them to deliver best practice in global policing for the benefit of the nation.

Well done to you.

Dr Charles Omole
2017

CHAPTER ONE

BRIEF HISTORICAL PERSPECTIVES OF POLICING IN NIGERIA

In historical African societies, policing was the job of all adults in village communities. Under the system of 'Hue, Cry and Pursuit' adults in communities were expected to be involved in control and crime prevention under the leadership of village and tribal elders.

But the emergence of the State structure with its vast bureaucracies and grasp for power, hierarchy and control changed the entrenched convention that policing is everybody's job.

There are several historical versions of the

evolution of the Nigeria police, but the central theme in these available materials relates to the strong-arm tactics of the colonial regime which required a ruthless force to deal with restless locals in order to enable ease of management of Nigeria as a colony.

Sir Stanhope Freeman, as the Governor of British West Africa, is generally credited with the foresight and initiative that created the initial group that later transformed into the police force of Nigeria[1]. Nwanze, posited:

> "Sir Freeman wrote a memo to the British Home Office requesting authority to create a force different from the Army to act as consular guards. His request was granted and the force, which he formed, was used to quell the Epe uprising of 1863. The activities of the guards drew the attention of the Governor of Lagos Colony, Captain

---

[1] Sam Nwanze, "In Thy Hands oh God: The Man, the Cop, the Preacher", Nio Publishers Lagos, 1999. P.79

John Glover. It was Captain Glover who requested and received permission of London to increase the number of the force to one hundred. Shortly after, the "Hausa Guard" and the Constabulary of the Lagos Colony were established. A legal instrument backed the new forces as an ordinance was enacted in 1879. This law was however amended with another ordinance, which created the Lagos Police Force, an investigative unit known as the criminal investigative department, in 1896".[2]

In his recorded account Tamuno[3] says that the Nigerian police originated between 1845 and 1861. With the colonial power's need for centralised control and compliance, a professionalised policing ethos was established to exert the state control, with or without the consent of the people.

---

[2] ibid
[3] Tekena Tamuno, The Police in Modern Nigeria 1861-1965, University Press Ibadan, 1970

In those days there were no distinction between the police and the military tactics when it came to the exertion of state hegemony and dominance. This created a militarised policing culture that has remained in many African societies till date.

According to Weber 1968,[4] the state gained the monopoly of legitimate violence and its delivery agents through the police in many nations, which in the case of African societies it was the continued colonial rule. Hence the police operated to secure the interest of the colonisers and not that of the colonised. This 'ruling class' focus of the early police organisation in Nigeria during the colonial era, many will say has not really changed in the post-colonial period.

Although its powers and operations are defined by laws, the practical operations of the police is affected by the political and socio-economic

---

[4] Weber, M. (1968) *Economy and Society*, university of California Press

interests of the governing elite and political groups in many nations. This fact was emphasised by Robert Reiner when he stated:

> "The police are the specialist carriers of the state's bedrock power: the monopoly of legitimate use of force. How and for what this is used speaks to the very heart of the condition of a political order. The danger of abuse, on behalf of particular partisan interests or the police themselves are clear and daunting".[5]

Hence it is posited that the more democratic a state is, the better the police will be at operating in the interest of the many rather than the few. As the police is a reflection of the state that controls it, an undemocratic state will be more oppressively policed for the benefit of the few.

Operational excellence in policing is easier in a

---

[5] Robert Reiner (1993) "Police Accountability: Principles, Patterns and Practices" in R. Reiner and S. Spencer (eds.) *Accountability Policing: Effectiveness, Empowerment and Equity* (London: Institute of public Policy Research).

state with advanced and developed democratic institutions and paradigm. Police were used by the colonial masters to brutally supress any opposition by the locals all over Nigeria. This started the negative perception of the police by Nigerians, a situation that has not changed after independence.

After securing home rule from the British in 1960, many expected a wholesome reorganisation of the police and its operating legal framework. That did not happen.

Instead a merely ceremonial transfer of service to local political leaders took place, leaving all the colonial statutes, ethos and legislative framework in place. This reality was left unchanged and some may say even made worse with decades of military dictatorships.

After independence, the Nigerian government accelerated the process of centralisation of the police, doing away with regional forces who were seen as badly trained, corrupt and political tools for local leaders.

Since the 1979 Constitution, there has been a provision for a national police force for the Nigerian state controlled from the centre. This was again affirmed in the 1999 Constitution.[6]

So the Nigerian state maintain a federal unified national police structure with each of the thirty-six states and Federal Capital City (FCT) Abuja having a police command led by a commissioner but controlled by the national leadership of the force.

POLICE POWERS AND LAWFUL FUNCTIONS

The duties and powers of the police are well articulated in the Police Act, 1943. Section 4 of the Act itemised the basic duties of the police as directly quoted below:[7]

- prevention and detection of crime
- apprehension of offenders

---

[6] Section 214(1)
[7] ibid

- preservation of law and order
- due enforcement of all laws and regulations with which they are directly, charged, and
- The performance of such other military duties within or outside Nigeria as may be required of them by or under the authority of the Act or any other Act. [8]

Additional powers and constitutional duties of the police included in the Act are:

- Power to conduct prosecutions in any court, subject to constitutional provision relating to the power of the Attorney-General of the Federation and of a state[9].
- Power to arrest without warrant in possession[10].
- Power to serve summons[11].
- Power to grant bail to a person arrested

---

[8] ibid
[9] S.25 of the Police Act
[10] ibid
[11] S.26 of the Police Act

without warrant[12].

- Power to issue search warrant by a superior officer[13].
- Power to take and record for purpose of identification and measurement, photographs and finger prints

With police powers comes responsibility as well. This is not different in Nigeria. Section 298 of the Criminal Procedure Code states that:

> "any person authorized by law to use force is criminally responsible for any excess according to the nature and quality of the act which is the excess"[14]

Additionally Section 374 (a,b) of the Police Regulations of 1968 allows for judicial oversight of police use of its powers.

Section 4 of the Police Act states that:

"The police shall be employed for the prevention and detection of crime, the

---

[12] S.27 of the Police Act
[13] S.28 of the Police Act
[14] The Criminal Procedure Code of Nigeria

apprehension of offenders, the preservation of law and order, the protection of life and property and the due enforcement of all laws and regulations with which they are charged and shall perform such military duties within or without Nigeria as may be required...[15]"

The police in Nigeria are empowered by law to carry out global standard policing duties and enforcement of the law and keeping of the peace. With mass poverty and high unemployment in Nigeria, along with the many operational challenges facing the police that is being examined in this book, police are seen as serving only the rich and powerful. They provide personal security to the rich and highly connected while the poor are largely left to fend for themselves and unprotected.

THE NIGERIA POLICE FORCE?
Decades after the end of colonialism; all of the military organisation in Nigeria seem to have been rebranded and adjusted to fit the nuances

---

[15] ibid

of Nigeria as a nation except for the police. That is why we have the **Nigerian** Army, the **Nigerian** Air force, the **Nigerian** Navy; but still have only the **Nigeria** Police Force.

Others have been Nigerianised (so to speak) except for the police that is still referred to as Nigeria (without the 'n') Police Force. This exemplify the almost colonial structure, approach, rules and mode of operation that still persists in the police. We need a Nigerian Police; a service that reflects the priorities and aspirations of the country. A service designed to best fit the peculiar landscape that the nation represents.

YOUR NOTES ON CHAPTER ONE

CHAPTER TWO

WHAT IS INTELLIGENCE-LED POLICING

Before stating the various definitions that has been formulated for Intelligence-led policing (ILP), I will like to use an illustration to best explain what ILP is all about. I will like to introduce you to the **Intelligent Elephant.**

Six blind men encounter an elephant. The first blind man touches the elephant's leg, and he says an elephant is like a pillar. The second blind man touches the elephant's tail, and he says, no, an elephant is like a rope.

The third blind man touches the elephant's trunk, and he says you're both crazy; an elephant is just like a tree branch. The fourth blind man touches the elephant's ear, and says he is certain that an elephant is like a hand held fan.

The fifth man touches the elephant's belly, and he insists that an elephant is like a wall. The sixth man touches the elephant's tusk, and he says, you are all wrong—an elephant is like a solid pipe! The men were arguing about the elephant when a sighted man came along and asked them what was wrong.

After they each told him what the elephant was like, he said, "You're all correct! An elephant has all the features you describe." This is the best way to illustrate ILP. This policing doctrine allows for each disjointed and separate pieces of data and information to be combined for a holistic and more meaningful picture to be created.

Intelligence is often referred to as a powerful tool in a law enforcement organization's arsenal. It has the capacity to provide command leaders with an operational picture of the environment that requires focused resources. Intelligence, as a structure, a process, and a product, is capable of strengthening a law enforcement organization's approach to better understanding the environment in which they police.

According to Lowenthal, intelligence refers to *"information that meets the stated or understood needs of policymakers and has been collected, refined, and narrowed to meet those needs. Intelligence is a subset of the broader category of information; intelligence and the entire process by which it is identified, obtained, and analysed respond to the needs of policymakers. All intelligence is information; not all information is intelligence".[16]*

In a South African White paper on Intelligence, it was defined as: *"the product resulting from the collection, evaluation, analysis, integration and interpretation of all available information, supportive of the policy and decision making processes pertaining to the national goals of stability, security and development".[17]*

Though often used interchangeably and incorrectly, there is a difference between information and intelligence. Unprocessed information helps raise awareness and understanding. When this information is analysed and evaluated, it becomes intelligence. Intelligence provides situational

---

[16] Mark M. Lowenthal. 2003. Intelligence: From Secrets to Policy. Washington, DC: CQ Press, p2
[17] Cited in Lauren Hutton. 2009. "Secrets, Spies, and Security", in L. Hutton (ed.) To spy or not to spy? Intelligence and democracy in South Africa. Pretoria: Institute of Security Studies, p.2

understanding that enables better decision making.

"Information + analysis = Intelligence".

What is ILP?
Intelligence-led policing (ILP) is a business process for systematically collecting, analysing, and utilising intelligence to guide law enforcement operational and tactical decisions.

ILP aids law enforcement in identifying, examining, and formulating preventative, protective, and responsive operations to specific targets, threats, and problems. It is important to note that ILP is not a new policing model; rather, it is an integrated enhancement (and deliberate Joined-up of isolated existing tools) that can contribute to public safety.

The concept of intelligence-led policing describes an emerging approach to policing that 'began to currency' (Smith 1997) in the early 1990s at the twilight of the 20th century.

The terrorist attack in New York on 9:11 is a vivid reminder of what happens when intelligence is kept in silos by different security agencies. Information on all the hijackers where on different databases of the various security agencies but none was talking to each other to help form a complete picture of the threats that existed.

So a complete picture was impossible. Many countries have since learned from that major error by trying to integrate and mine all their data and intelligence in joined up ways. But this is not the case in Nigeria.

The ILP process can provide a meaningful contribution by supporting the Police's existing policing strategy, whether it is community-oriented policing, problem-oriented policing, or other methodology.

The ability to collect, examine, vet, and compare vast quantities of information enables law enforcement agencies to understand crime patterns and identify individuals, enterprises, and locations that represent the highest threat to the community and concentration of criminal and/or terrorist-related activity.

The most extensive and insightful definition of the ILP was given by Smith as follows:

"Intelligence-led policing is a term that has only begun to gain currency in the last three to five years. For this reason, it lacks a single overarching definition. Most would agree, however, that at its most fundamental, intelligence-led policing involves the collection and analysis of information to produce an intelligence end product designed to inform police decision-making at both tactical and strategic levels. It is a model of policing in which intelligence serves as a guide to operations, rather than the reverse. It is innovative and, by some standards, even radical, but it is predicated on the notion that a principal task of the police is to prevent and detect crime rather than react to it".[18]

Through this method, the Police can prioritise the deployment of resources in a manner that efficiently achieves the greatest crime-reduction and prevention outcomes. (Like all other security agencies, the Police must prioritise to be more effective).

Intelligence has always been part of police work. However, in the traditional policing approach, intelligence is used to aid investigation after a crime incident. This approach has been referred to as policing-led intelligence (Cope 2004). In contrast, intelligence-led policing (ILP) repositions intelligence from back-stage to front-stage of policing. This is necessary as emphasis is now in guaranteeing and preserving public safety

---

[18] Smith, A. 1997. Intelligence Led Policing: International Perspectives on Policing in the 21st Century. Lawrenceville, New Jersey: International Association of Law Enforcement Intelligence Analysts, Inc.

has moved away from mere enforcement to risk and crime prevention. So intelligence is supposed to direct the actions of the police in a more accurate fashion.

ILP encourages the use of both overt and covert information gathering. This approach also maximizes the use of available resources and partnerships, such as those capabilities available through informants, the civic society and local/State intelligence centres.

The reasons for the rapid development and enthusiastic adoption of some form of ILP model in developed economies and polities have been identified by one of the world leading scholars in this area as follow:

a) the desire to explore new approaches to crime control;
b) ineffectiveness of the standard model of policing.

c) paucity of evidence that a reactive and investigative approach to policing has any impact on the level of crime;

d) financial constraints imposed on police departments during the rapid increases in recorded crime in the 1970s and 1980s;

e) availability of new technologies that increased the volume of information and capacity of information retrieval and analysis services available to police chiefs, helped spur interest in analytical approaches to problem identification and definition commonly known problem oriented policing;

f) lack of convincing evidence that community policing is effective in reducing crime;

g) problem-oriented policing lacks the evidentiary base for widespread adoption.[19]

---

[19] Ratcliffe, JH and Guidetti 2008. State police investigative structure and the adoption of intelligence led policing. Policing: An International Journal of Police Strategies & Management, Vol. 31 No. 1: 109-128

ILP is executive implementation of the intelligence cycle to support proactive decision making for resource allocation and crime prevention. In order to successfully implement this business process, Zonal leadership must have clearly defined priorities as part of their policing strategy.

At its core, ILP helps leaders make informed decisions to address policing priorities. These priorities can include issues such as crime prevention, crime reduction, case management, resource allocation, case clearance, anticipation of future threats, or crime problems. This process provides guidance and support to the Police leadership, regardless of the type of priority established.

ILP Operational Concept

For ILP to work, there has to be Steering from the Leadership on the following:

- A clearly defined Priorities
- The Policing Strategy

Individual junior officers CANNOT be expected to lead on ILP, although they are needed to implement it. This is a crucial point to note.

There is no single method for implementing ILP. The size of the State Command, complexity of the threat environment, the local political environment, and resource availability within each command varies greatly across the Zonal commands on the Nigerian police.

Therefore, how ILP implementation "looks" within each State or Zone may vary accordingly. (E.g, a very rural command can rely more on human Intelligence, while another in urban area may rely more of technology sourced intelligence). However, adopting ILP as a philosophy and business framework, to whatever degree is appropriate, can and will improve the effectiveness and efficiency of any policing organization.

The end goal of ILP is to enhance proactive policing efforts and further the positive outcomes of law enforcement actions toward reducing crime and protecting the community against a variety of threats.

Accountability

ILP has an extremely high potential for abuse. Hence need for up to date training for ALL officers.

There is a tendency, even in democratic countries, for ILP organizations to abuse their powers or even to operate outside the law because many organizations involved in ILP are granted extensive intelligence access. But our society must possess a police force governed by the rule of law.

In some countries, for example, ILP organizations regularly engage in actions of dubious legality, such as arbitrarily arresting and detaining people without charge, without legal representation, and without means of communication; some high-policing forces also engage in torture. This is why senior leadership steer and oversight is essential.

Benefits of ILP

The overall benefit of ILP is that it supports police operations so that it can focus its limited resources as effectively as possible, to achieve the greatest crime prevention and reduction outcomes.

ILP enables the Police to move with the trends and evolving pattern of Criminal activities. ILP enables Pro-activity from the police instead of just being Reactive. ILP creates an Integrated overview of what the police know within its Silos.

The goal of a good ILP implementation according to J H Ratcliffe is to focus on the three I's. These are:
- INTERPRETING the environment
- INFLUENCING management and
- Creating the desired IMPACT on crime and criminality.

This model provides police management and commanders with Actionable Intelligence products that will allow them to understand and effectively respond.

CHAPTER SUMMARY

1. ILP though recent, is not a new Policing method.
2. ILP is new way to make existing Policing methods and tools more effective.
3. ILP requires Leadership from the Top.
4. ILP requires officers to begin to Think differently.
5. ILP requires Joined-Up ways of working.
6. ILP is the future of Policing as funding fails to catch-up with demands on the Police.
7. ILP requires Strategic thinking, not just Tactical.

YOUR NOTES ON CHAPTER TWO

CHAPTER THREE

UNDERSTANDING AND IMPLEMENTING INTELLIGENCE-LED POLICING

The operation of ILP policy centres around certain key principles that helps the policing organisation to understand what intelligence-led policing is all about.

Successful implementation and sustainment of the ILP framework within the police require strong commitment by the State, Zonal and National leadership. ILP cannot be implemented without a top down push by the police leadership.

The leaders should be able to clearly articulate the goals of ILP: how it will address the command's priorities, how it will affect police operations, and how the police will benefit from its use.

Leaders must lead by example—fully integrating intelligence into their strategic, operational, and tactical decisions— thereby demonstrating their confidence in the ILP approach and providing evidence of how using intelligence leads to better decisions.

ILP requires major Cultural SHIFT in individual police officer. Each officer must begin to think Multilaterally. This represents a significant challenge in the ethos of policing in Nigeria. Silo thinking and individualized command focus must give way to Zonal/Sub-national cooperation and Intelligence sharing.

Creating cultural change is difficult and requires strong, consistent leadership from the police leadership. Reward system and acknowledgements must include contributors and not just the final solvers. If six officers contributed information that leads to an eventual capture of a criminal; all six (contributors) should be acknowledged, not just the arresting officer (solver). The habit of police commands in Nigeria is to only recognise the arresting officer or team, while ignoring all those that contributed intelligence and information along the way.

It requires changing attitudes, values, and beliefs about policing processes and redefining organizational procedures, including how personnel view crime problems, how information is shared, and how to integrate threat prevention with crime prevention.

TOOLS TO OPERATIONALISE ILP

After making a decision to implement ILP within a command, zone or even nationally, certain tools must be put in place to operationalise this leadership intent. I will like us to look at some of these essential tools.

Top Leadership Commitment

There are several things the Leadership can do to implement and institutionalize ILP at any command level. Firstly, the leadership need to develop a vision that is founded upon ILP. A mission statement need to be crafted that is rooted in ILP. Once this is done, then the real work starts. That is communicating this vision to the rank and file.

The national leadership need to communicate the vision to all the zonal and state commands leadership team. This cannot be done by just sending a signal to them. This will require a team meeting or retreat. The leaders need to be left in no doubt about the mission and goal to pursue ILP.

There is then a need to educate and incorporate the state command senior team so they understand and "buy into" the vision, as they will be instrumental in creating the final implemented processes. Communicate to all levels of the state command and demonstrate how the intelligence provided through the ILP approach works to address the state's top priorities.

The police top leadership, must encourage the rank and file by demonstrating how ILP help inform their decision and bolster their policy making framework. So, the top leadership must continuously lead by example by showing officers how analysis and intelligence products are used to make strategic, operational, and tactical decisions at the highest level.

Top leaders must ensure that ILP gets concrete sufficient and ongoing support (not just mere words) to achieve full implementation. This includes the assignment of personnel and resources to fulfil the police ILP framework.

Police chiefs also have to promote crime and intelligence analysis. The integration of the intelligence and crime analysis function is essential to uncovering crimes linked to organised groups of criminals.

To roll out ILP nationally; a zonal implementation strategy approach should be employed by the Nigeria Police Force. The Zonal Commands should be the hubs for implementing ILP.

A taskforce should be instituted in each zone to lead and run with the implementation of ILP. A zonal specific ILP framework need to be produced. This will involve the documentation of each zone's threat and criminal activity priorities as specific to each commands. Then a strategic plan to address the priorities need to be produced by each zonal taskforce.

Each zone will need to identify its intelligence capabilities and leverage existing resources, such as emergency calls operators, to avoid duplication of efforts. Then there is need to organize an intelligence apparatus or leverage another's (partner agencies) to collect, analyse, and develop intelligence to address the identified priorities. Finally, the taskforce then need to prepare each zone to implement

ILP through training, education, and awareness.

For officers in the field, ILP requires becoming both better data collectors and better consumers of intelligence-related products. This means shifting from emphasising post-event evidence collection to constantly gathering all relevant data and ensuring it is provided for entry into appropriate databases, as well as drawing from the intelligence analysts and relevant databases all the information that is needed to support ongoing operations. NO MORE SILOS.

For support officers and back office staff, the key components of the ILP process include the creation of tactical, operational, and strategic intelligence products that support immediate needs, promote situational awareness, and provide the foundation for longer-term planning. I will address the issue of intelligence products later in this chapter.

Collaboration and Coordination

In order to implement ILP and make efficient resource allocation decisions, Nigerian police must collaborate and coordinate with other information sharing partners. It is critical that existing resources be leveraged.

Partner agencies and other stakeholders are also a main component of ILP implementation. They often have a unique, strategic understanding of the community that will provide additional information and intelligence. Frequent and ongoing communications with all of the zonal ILP stakeholders is vital for success.

Receiving a broad base of input from internal and external stakeholders will contribute to the integrity of the design for the ILP function. (An Inward Looking Police ethos will not promote ILP operation).

Interacting with other members of the Law Enforcement community (e.g DSS), Criminal Justice System (e.g Prisons) and public safety communities (e.g LASTMA in Lagos) will create valuable conduits for future information and intelligence sharing. Cooperation, partnerships, and effective two-way information sharing are key components of successful ILP.

It is important that all the Zonal Commands update or implement a privacy policy that addresses their information sharing processes. This policy should clearly address how the ILP framework is utilised.

Intelligence interface is needed with :

- ➤ **INTRA ZONAL UNITS** – States within the Zonal command
- ➤ **THE PUBLIC SECTOR** – E.g Other Security agencies
- ➤ **THE PRIVATE SECTOR** – E.g Telephone Companies.
- ➤ **THE COMMUNITY** – E.g Churches, Mosques etc.
- ➤ **THE GENERAL PUBLIC**

ILP need to be fed with information from many channels to be effective. So cooperation with other agencies of government is essential.

Command Tasking & Coordination

Fundamentally, it is necessary to view ILP as a core management philosophy of the command and control functions of the police. This allows commanders, DPOs and officers in the field to understand, adopt, and value a centralised tasking and coordination function required for advancing ILP.

The police have to balance a myriad of duties and responsibilities in their jurisdictions. This often presents unique challenges for command personnel on where to expend resources and focus operations. A robust tasking and coordination system will allow the zones to synchronize these efforts by aligning personnel and resources toward strategic, operational, and tactical goals.

The following FOUR approaches can be adopted by the zonal commands for building a tasking and coordination function within its operational divisions:

- Direct analytical resources to produce a Baseline threat assessment for the Zone, (If none exists).
- Use the threat assessment to identify command/zonal priorities.
  - Zone-wide centrally mandated priorities, or
  - Divisional/State level priorities mandated by the Zonal HQ
- Establish a tasking and coordination group to assist command-level staff.
- Coordinate a monthly or quarterly tasking and coordination meeting among Divisional commanders and Zonal Headquarters team to:
  - Identify intelligence and investigative gaps with regard to outreach, patrol, enforcement, and investigative initiatives.
  - Coordinate resource allocation and effort.

o Task personnel concerning intelligence and investigative initiatives. (Announce Zonal agreed updated priorities)
o Ensure that command priorities are being carried out.

Collection and Planning of Information

The capacity for a police division or State command to collect pertinent information is vital to an ILP framework. The various zones, state and divisional commands should ensure that they have the ability to collect information from the following sources:

> Open sources
> Community outreach
> Acquisition and analysis of physical evidence
> Interviews and interrogation
> Financial investigations
> Surveillance
> Informants
> Electronic surveillance
> Undercover operations

The daily interaction that officers have with the community in terms of community-policing efforts, motor vehicle stops, and calls for service, offers them a unique ability to **gather information that may lead to identifying suspicious activity** related to criminal or terrorist operations.

However, to ensure that collection activities are focused, they should be guided by:

> ➤ Analytical needs (*Clarifying existing Information*)
> ➤ Intelligence requirements. *(Bigger haystack is not always good)*
> ➤ Investigative needs
> ➤ Threat identification

The tasking and coordination group identified within the previous section can ensure that collection efforts within a command are focused and conducted in a manner that is legal and ethical and adds value to the ILP effort.

Command Analytic Capabilities

In order for ILP to be successful, Zonal command leadership must assist Divisional commanders **to develop and improve their** analytic capability to support the centrally mandated priorities. These capabilities support the decision-making process by providing the right information to the right person, at the right time. There are several steps in the development of these capabilities, including:

1) **COLLECTION PLAN STRATEGY.** A collection plan identifies priority information that should be collected/ gathered, outlines the process for gathering relevant information from all law enforcement sources, and describes how that information is developed into an intelligence product.

> ➢ Information collected is analyzed using the **intelligence cycle,** and the reliable information is developed into intelligence

products used to monitor and address the strategic priorities.

The production of criminal intelligence is accomplished by following the six steps of the intelligence cycle — planning and direction, collection, processing/collation, analysis, dissemination, and revaluation.

The intelligence cycle[20] used by the intelligence community is the foundation of the ILP framework; therefore, it is imperative to understand and follow each step in the cycle in order to develop and sustain an effective and efficient intelligence function.

Step 1: Planning and Direction — Define intelligence requirements and develop an intelligence unit mission statement to guide intelligence efforts.

---

[20] The Geneva Centre for the Democratic Control of Armed Forces (DCAF). 2006. Intelligence services. DCAF Backgrounder. Geneva: DCAF

Step 2: Collection—Gather raw data from multiple sources, including field reports, open source records, the Internet, citizen accounts, informants, covert operations, and the media.

Step 3: Processing/Collation — Evaluate the validity and reliability of the information; sort, combine, categorize, and arrange the data so relationships can be detected.

Step 4: Analysis — Connect information in a logical and meaningful way to produce intelligence reports that contain valid judgments based on analysed information.

Step 5: Dissemination — Share timely, credible intelligence with other law enforcement, public safety, and private sector individuals/entities that have a right and need to know.

Step 6: Re-evaluation — Evaluate the process performed and the products produced to assess effectiveness, efficiency, relevancy, and weaknesses.

There are several steps in the development of these capabilities, so after collection plan development strategy, a few additional steps are needed to enhance the analytic capabilities of the zonal commands.

2) **ANALYSIS** - As dictated by the collection plan, information is transformed into intelligence through analysis. This analysis connects the data through the linking of incidents, activities, or behaviours. *The goal of analysis is to produce intelligence products that help the Zonal decision makers identify potential or future threats, respond to relevant threats, understand potential issues, and plan for proactive action.*

3) **INTELLIGENCE PRODUCTS** — Providing a mechanism to communicate the results of the analytic process,

intelligence products are a key element in the ILP process. Police will use a **variety of intelligence products**, including reports, briefings, and multimedia presentations. The effectiveness of intelligence reports is directly related to the quality of the information and analysis used.

4) **OPERATIONAL RESPONSES** — The intelligence products better equip the zonal decision makers to provide operational direction and command. These products may help identify where potential threats currently exist or may occur; it is the decision maker's responsibility to develop an operational mitigation or response strategy.

5) **REVIEW OF THE PROCESS** — Evaluation of the analytical process helps identify any new or emerging information gaps. The Zonal ILP efforts will benefit from knowing whether the analytical process is addressing the

appropriate issues, at the appropriate time, for the appropriate purpose.

Education and Continuous Training

Training police personnel requires a coordinated, force-wide approach that involves daily awareness and education regarding the goals and objectives of ILP. Using information from the training activities, decision makers should educate all of the rank and file regarding information collection and sharing tenets as well as appropriate measures to safeguard and handle information.

The Police decision makers should, at a minimum, obtain training regarding the intelligence process, indicators and warnings regarding potential criminal or terrorist activity, legal and privacy issues, and information sharing networks and resources.

As the zones adopt ILP, it is important that they implement a privacy policy, or if there is an existing policy, it should be reviewed and, if necessary, amended to ensure the protection of individuals' privacy, civil rights, and civil liberties so that they correspond with the ILP approach.

Additionally, these policies and procedures should be reinforced throughout each zone so that divisional officers and other personnel understand the importance and sensitivity of these issues.

Feedback & Reassessment

One method of evaluating the success of the ILP implementation is to review end-user feedback concerning the process. End users come in a variety of forms, including the backroom officers who receives the raw data from the field, the zonal command officers who reviews the analytical product, the Commissioners and zonal leadership team who reviews intelligence products, and the officers in the field who receives orders based on the conclusions drawn from the intelligence.

Each user has a unique perspective to provide. Incorporating this feedback into the evaluation process will help the zones improve their ILP process by continuously providing new information on which processes and products can advance.

Each zonal leadership team should use an evaluation process to assess whether activities are being performed in a manner consistent with the identified strategic priorities.

Using performance measures will provide a consistent method of evaluating program development progress. This evaluation will determine whether the zone's implementation of ILP is successful or whether adjustments to the ILP strategy need to made.

Leaders must constantly evaluate the ILP outcomes to determine whether the implementation has allowed each Zone to address its priorities. If so, the existing priorities must be adjusted to accommodate this accomplishment. If not, the ILP strategy should be fine tuned.

This includes the identification of gaps throughout the process and a method to address and solve the identified issues.

YOUR NOTES ON CHAPTER THREE

CHAPTER FOUR

POLICING AND INTELLIGENCE OPERATIONS IN NIGERIA

We will discuss the challenges facing the implementation of Intelligence-led policing (ILP) in Nigeria in the next Chapter, but in this chapter I will like us to briefly examine the policing culture in Nigeria as it relates to intelligence gathering and exploitation.

As detailed in the next Chapter, Nigeria has too many agencies that acquires domestic intelligence on its behalf. This disparate nature of these agencies makes a unified intelligence architecture difficult in Nigeria. What we have are silos of information and the dots are not joined, especially since there is absence of a compelling unifying legislative framework to make joined-up working compulsory.

Nigeria has four major intelligence agencies and several intelligence units within the law enforcement agencies. The four major agencies are:

1) the **State Security Service** (primarily responsible for internal state security intelligence and operations);

2) **Criminal Intelligence Bureau** of the Nigeria Police Force (with responsibility for crime intelligence);

3) **National Intelligence Agency** (responsible for the external intelligence interests of the nation) and

4) the **Defence Intelligence Agency** (charged with defence intelligence)

It is a fact that criminal activities do not respect the finely defined line of duties of these agencies. A major criminal activity can have national defence implication as well as international dimension to it. So who is responsible for gathering such intelligence; given the cross-agency nature of the problem. This is where the lack of effective joined-up operations between these agencies creates a problem for effective ILP.

There is, at present, no effective and efficient professional institutional framework for the coordination of these agencies. Existing channels of interagency coordination are the Office of the National Security Adviser and the Joint Intelligence Board. But these are not effective as presently operated and the focus of these channels tend to be more political and terror related instead of criminality.

Accordingly, for the purpose of ILP, the criminal intelligence operations will be most paramount. Budgetary constraints however restrict the ability of the police and other agencies to secure some high quality intelligence in certain operations.

A senior police source narrated an example of

how lack of funds to conduct decent intelligence operations handicaps the police. The source stated that the police was tracking a known drug trafficker with the aim of collecting actionable intelligence that can be used for prosecution.

The suspect lodged himself in a suite at a top hotel in Abuja, Nigeria. The best practice would have been for the police to book the suite next door and listen in on the suspect from there.

But the police command could not find the funds to pay for the suite next door. Hence the police could only listen in and track the suspect while in public places around the hotel.

They gave up after a few days when it became clear that the suspect never discussed anything of interest while in public areas. This is just an example of how lack of funds is eroding the capacity of the police to deliver on its legal mandate to protect the public and prosecute criminals through effective intelligence-led operation.

There is a common saying in policing circle that *'good intelligence leads to good case. Bad intelligence leads to bad case. No intelligence leads to no case'.* This is not only true, but explains the poor rate of crime resolution in Nigeria.

HIGH v LOW POLICING[21]

There are many definitions of High Policing as it relates to Political policing and the maintenance of state Dominance over its people. In its original meaning it referred to the use of political intelligence to preserve the power of the ruler, in particular as this involved stealth, spying, espionage and intrigue.

Yet, like barnacles that become attached to a ship, over time the concept has evolved and layers of meaning have been added. But for this book, we will concentrate on a narrower

---

[21] J Brodeur, (1983) ' High Policing and Low Policing', *Social Problems*, 30/5: 507-20.

aspect of this Paradigm.

High policing refers to matters of organised criminality, coordinated threats and activities threatening the security of the state. This tends to be pro-active activities like surveillance, intelligence gathering and undercover infiltration of the criminal communities.

Additionally, High policing is a form of intelligence-led policing that serves to protect the national government or a conglomerate of national governments from internal threats; that is, any policing operations integrated into domestic intelligence gathering, national security, or international security operations

The primary tool of high policing is intelligence, which is derived from both human and technological sources. Intelligence-Led Policing (ILP) can be construed to be a part of High policing doctrine.

Nigerian police focus too much on 'Low"

policing at the expense of "High Policing. Low policing refers to the everyday routine protection of citizens. This is largely reactive policing based on either notification of ongoing criminality or after the criminal act have been committed. High policing on the other hand refers to matters threatening to the security of the state.

This tend to be pro-active activities like surveillance, intelligence gathering and undercover infiltration of the criminal communities. This is not to say that the Nigerian police do the low policing well either. It is just that the high policing is largely non existent as a practice. The skills, competence, capacity and funds required for sustained high level policing is not present in the police as currently constituted.

Prevention and detection of crime is a prerequisite to effective policing. Intelligence gathering is key to crime detection. Habitually, it seems the police in Nigeria arrest to investigate rather than investigate to arrest. This is what I call laid back or lazy policing.

Their investigatory focus tends to be specific crime informed. So a career armed robber who is arrested based on a suspected act; will be questioned only about that particular crime as that is the focus. Instead of an intelligence-led approach of mining the suspects for all data he possesses that will assist in solving many other crimes.

Many factors are responsible for this sorry state of policing culture in Nigeria:

- o Lack of modern equipment including communications and forensic Infrastructure due to funding constraints. This means that officers still largely depend on rudimentary methods to investigate crime.
- o There is also shortage of highly trained officers, especially amongst the rank and file of the police command.

Continuous professional training of the rank and file is practically non-existent in the Nigeria police. There are officers with training briefs who do not conduct any training for years on end. All blame paucity of funds for this sorry state of affairs.

o Police officers are routinely accused of abuse, torture, cruel inhuman and degrading treatment of suspects in their custody. To these officers, ILP is not even in their consideration.

o Lack of effective inter-agency cooperation amongst the myriads of policing related agencies in Nigeria is also a problem.

Policing by Consent

A fundamental thesis of effective policing is that the cooperation and support of majority of the citizens exist to assist the police in its work. This is the doctrine of policing by consent. But with the bad reputation of the police in Nigeria, public assistance is rarely forthcoming. This makes the task of intelligence gathering much more difficult. There are some historical foundation for this distrust in the police-public relationship.

In a functioning democracy, policing is usually by consent of the citizens. They count on the goodwill and cooperation of the public in carrying out their duties. The Nigerian police with its militarised colonial origin and decades of military rule have become alienated from the people and seen merely as an oppressive tool in the hands of government.

In his recorded account Tamuno[22] says that the Nigerian police originated between 1845 and 1861. With the colonial power's need for centralised control and compliance, a professionalised policing ethos was established to exert the state control, with or without the consent of the people.

In those days there were no distinction

---

[22] Tekena Tamuno, The Police in Modern Nigeria 1861-1965, University Press Ibadan, 1970

between the police and the military tactics when it came to the exertion of state hegemony and dominance. This created a militarised policing culture that has remained in many African societies till date.

According to Weber 1968,[23] the state gained the monopoly of legitimate violence and its delivery agents through the police in many nations, which in the case of African societies it was the continued colonial rule. Hence the police operated to secure the interest of the colonisers and not that of the colonised. This 'ruling class' focus of the early police organisation in Nigeria during the colonial era, many will say has not really changed in the post-colonial period.

To become effective at ILP, the police need to earn and gain the trust of the people. The citizens are a treasure throve of intelligence for the police if they are happy with their police and

---

[23] [23] Weber, M. (1968) *Economy and Society,* university of California Press

the way it performs its role. The principle of consent in policing is therefore essential to secure public buy-in into police activities.

The principle of intelligence-led policing describes how knowledge and understanding of criminal threats and patterns are used to drive law enforcement actions in response to threat of organized crime.

Globalisation of Criminality

Apart from the national intelligence challenges we have been looking at; there is also the globalisation of criminality factor that has made crime and threats to take on a transnational or multinational dimension. This requires an internationalised intelligence operation and cooperation which is currently not the norm in Nigeria.

Among such international crimes are terrorism, corruption and money laundering, human trafficking, drug trafficking, theft of mineral resources, weapons smuggling and trade in fake and substandard products and pharmaceuticals, amongst others. As a result, these crimes require proactive measures rather than reactive approach which is the traditional policing model in Nigeria because when they occur, the consequences are often destructive.

In Nigeria, Intelligence-led operation is the exception not the rule. There are many officers who do not seem to see the value or benefit of intelligence-led approach, which can be detailed and laborious or even sometimes banal.

The acquisition of knowledge for the policing of these global cross-border crimes requires dynamic engagement and partnership among security and intelligence agencies as well as between law enforcement agencies and critical non-law enforcement stakeholders within and across nations.

It is in this context that it is often stated that contemporary major crimes require transnational network and intelligence-led policing.

Inter-agency rivalry is also a limiting factor in Nigeria. Training of officers is also a factor. Training is one thing the Nigerian police do very badly in. The quality, detail and frequency of professional training is inadequate within the police.

Operational v Strategic Intelligence

A distinction has been drawn between operational intelligence and strategic intelligence – each with different aims. While operational intelligence is typically short-term in nature, strategic intelligence focuses on the long-term aims and objectives of law enforcement agencies.

As *Robertson* has pointed out aptly;
"although operational and strategic intelligence analyses have different aims, they are mutually dependent ... attempts to separate them, or to

foster one at the expense of the other, will result in a fundamentally flawed intelligence programme and a failure to generate meaningful assessments of criminal activity".[24]

Operational intelligence is an integral part of the legal framework for policing in Nigeria is provided in the Criminal Procedure Act (CPA).[25]

CPA provides that:
"Notwithstanding the provisions of this or any other written law relating to arrest, a police officer knowing of a design to commit any offence may arrest, without orders from a magistrate and without a warrant, the person so designing, if it appears to such officer that the commission of the offence cannot otherwise be prevented."[26]

---

[24] Robertson, Simon, Intelligence-led Policing: a European Union view in Intelligence-Led Policing: International Perspectives on Policing in the 21st Century, published by International Association of Law Enforcement Intelligence Analysts Incorporated, September 1997, pp.21-23.
[25] Section 55 Criminal Procedure Act (CPA).
[26] ibid

Therefore, the law allows the police to act based on either Operational or strategic intelligence to effect an arrest in prevention of crime and safety of the public.

YOUR NOTES ON CHAPTER FOUR

CHAPTER FIVE

CHALLENGES TO
INTELLIGENCE-LED POLICING
IN NIGERIA

Policing Nigeria seems to be getting harder for the Nigeria Police Force (NPF) due to the misguided agendas of some politicians who seem bent on destroying whatever is left of the operational effectiveness of the police.

The NPF has been under attack since the mid-70s when the military administration, removed the Special Branch out of the Force and made it a separate independent organisation. The Special Branch later became the NSO during

Shagari administration and then changed its name to the SSS of today.

Although its powers and operations are defined by laws, the practical operation of the Nigerian police is affected by the political and socio-economic interests of the governing elite and political groups in Nigeria.

The 1999 Constitution of the Federal Republic of Nigeria in section 214 (1) states that:

"There shall be a Police Force for Nigeria, which shall be known as the Nigeria Police Force and subject to the provisions of this section, no other Police Force shall be established for the Federation or any part thereof".

Section 214 (2)(a) empowers the National Assembly to produce an Act to organise and administer the details of police operations in Nigeria in ways that protects the constitutional rights of Nigerians. This is known as the Police

Act. First enacted in 1943, it has been reviewed by the legislature in 1967 and 1979. A new review is being planned by the National Assembly.

This constitutional provision makes it unconstitutional for either the government of the states or even the federal government to establish a parallel police service in competition to the Nigeria police Force. This has however not stopped the Federal government from establishing additional investigatory and enforcement institutions, even though they have not called any of them 'police'.

Many in government agree that the Nigerian government seem to be in breach of the spirit of the constitution if not the letter of it. By not calling these parallel agencies "police" the government seem to say they have stayed within the provisions of the law. But with these agencies having powers similar to that of the police and taking over functions and duties performed by the police, it can be argued that if it looks like a dog, barks like a dog, walks like a dog, then it is a dog.

These agencies perform policing duties, hence it can be argued that they are police in practice if not in names. But nobody has yet litigated this fact by taking the government to a court of competent jurisdiction over it. Examples of these additional agencies are:

1. The Federal Road Safety Commission (FRSC)
2. The Economic and Financial Crime Commission (EFCC)
3. The Independent Corrupt Practices Commission (ICPC)
4. The National Security and Civil Defence Corps (NSCDC)
5. The Code of Conduct Bureau (CCB)
6. Vehicle Inspection Office (VIO)
7. State Security Service (SSS)
8. National Drug Law Enforcement Agency (NDLEA)

For instance, the CCT has not led to accelerated hearings of misconduct cases, hence there is doubt as to its continued existence.

Most in the Police believe the plethora of agencies, many with overlapping powers, and duplicated duties have led to the weakening of the main police force as a result of talent flight to these new agencies and reduction in police funding, as funds are allocated to these additional agencies.

Having multiple agencies is not the entire problem in itself; but when they are badly formed with unclear remit and overlapping duties and no legislative mandate to integrate databases; it becomes a recipe for disaster and disincentive to ILP implementation.

The main police force is then left to do the heavy lifting task of crime prevention and investigation with fewer resources to do the job. These policing related agencies consume a lot of resources and many believe overwhelmingly they are inefficient and incoherent in operational agility. These many policing agencies stretches the budget of the government to the detriment of the NPF.

We are now in a situation where the Federal government only manages to pay the emoluments of the police officers and barely nothing else is available for equipment, training etc, thus the operational funding of the police now largely come from the goodwill of the respective state governments. As a result, a multi-tier police is emerging.

With states like Lagos able to better support the police and others like Adamawa doing much less. If this trend continues; the federal government will lose its moral right to a federal police structure it cannot afford to fund.

From nowhere, President Obasanjo created the Civil Defence corps and put his cronies' in it. Billions of naira were spent establishing this group to perform duties meant for the Nigeria Police constitutionally. Few people see any value this group brought to the nation. But in the meantime, Billions meant for the Police has now been diverted to another agency created by politicians.

Given the foregoing, one will wonder why the National Assembly is now creating another paramilitary group called the Peace Corps.[27] It does not make sense. That will make it the ninth agency to be created to perform a traditional police function. If this Peace Corps bill is finally passed by the National Assembly, Nigeria will now have TEN organisations performing policing duties; including the main NPF itself. This is madness.

Effective policing in most countries is made of a unified police body that has specialist units within it to focus on special areas of security interests, but all under the same command and control system and sharing unified databases

---

[27] Under consideration as at March 2017

for joined up intelligence-led policing. Instead of this, Nigeria seems to be creating more policing agencies and inevitable confusion of roles, duplicated responsibility; unclear hierarchy of power amongst them and financial dissipation that makes the NPF suffer under little or no funding.

With the Peace corps, we have Ten policing organisations, Ten Back-office departments and cost centres, ten databases, ten operational procedures and intelligence systems and a massively confused citizenry who are now not sure who to call on amongst all these policing agencies.

In all countries I know of if a civil servant steals; you call the police. In Nigeria, we created the ICPC. Why? With these kaleidoscope of policing organisations, you also have Ten prosecuting agencies for relatively similar crimes. This creates multiple prosecution standards and inconsistent prosecutorial decisions.

In the end, it seems the politicians are only interested in creating power bases for themselves in the security sector of the country.

This is to aid their manipulation of our laws and impunity in political activities. The solution is to unify all these agencies under the NPF, strengthen our police, fund them better and demand better outcomes accordingly.

The trend globally in the security sector is to join-up activities of different agencies and reduce their number to the barest minimum. We seem to be going in the opposite direction. You can finish serving a jail sentence for robbery in Niger state and travel to Lagos the next day to join the Police. There is no national database of criminals in Nigeria.

The system relies on the honesty of applicants to declare their own past convictions. In fact, there is no State-wide database of criminals in any state. All we have is a state-wide record of cases, not criminals. And this is mainly manual when it exists.

So if there is no joined-up operation within the police as a result of a paucity of funds and historical neglect; how much more cooperation will exist between the police and all these other policing organisations on criminal intelligence gathering.

Historically, while the military invested and modernise themselves infrastructure wise when they were in power, the police was deliberately underfunded and neglected. So the continuing negative public perception of the role and capacity of the police is a major source of concern in a democracy.

Hence the Nigerian police remain the most misunderstood profession by the general public in Nigeria. Many expect them to work magic despite the limitations and massive constraints of their tools and service conditions. Their performance is weighed with misconception and ignorance, resulting in an out of context assessment of their activities.

Ignorance of the inner workings of the police and the penchant for secrecy by the Nigeria police had led to little public confidence in the service by Nigerians, plenty of misconception and depleted public support and cooperation with the police. These challenges are being exacerbated by the plethora of policing agencies created by the politicians. These other agencies create a capacity problem for the police and dilute the funding available to the NPF.

The foregoing scenario make Intelligence-led policing almost impossible to implement in Nigeria. With ten policing organisations, ten databases and ten different chains of command; it is a recipe for chaos and confusion. So the main obstacle to ILP in Nigeria is the fragmented policing agencies that do not cooperate effectively and creates silos of information that has not been processed in a holistic way to give clarity to leadership on what action to take in any particular instance.

So an amalgamation of some if not all of these policing agencies may be a necessary step before the full benefit of ILP can be enjoyed by the Nigeria Police Force.

In my opinion; it is now time we create a unified criminal security platform in Nigeria under the leadership of the NPF as the only constitutionally empowered civil security organisation. Train them, strengthen them, support them and see a new security landscape emerge that we all can be proud of.

The police as presently crafted and treated by the politicians is set up to fail. We need the leadership of the National Assembly to see the need for a joined-up security infrastructure and unified command and control. Creating the Peace Corps must be abandoned and the funds meant for it given to the Nigerian police to strengthen its numbers and operational tools.

There are many challenges associated with implementing ILP. As stated earlier, there is no one type of ILP implementation. Although this makes the framework flexible for use in all types of Policing situation like we have in Nigeria, it also provides some potential impediments, including:

1. **Sequence of Implementation.** Deciding the order of ILP implementation can be a daunting task. Police commands with limited existing analytical functions may see this approach as overwhelming. But attempt must be made to follow best practice on as many occasions as possible.

2. **Perception of a complicated analytical function.** ILP does have a significant analytical component; however, not all police commands will employ all of the available analytical capabilities. Divisional commanders can

adopt analytical tactics that are relevant and necessary to meet their specific needs; unless this becomes a centralised national function.

3. **Human Resources.** Rather than requiring additional manpower, ILP supports the existing staff by providing better intelligence to make more informed decisions. ILP allows the zonal command manpower to be utilised in a coordinated fashion based on empirical knowledge that supports the zonal priorities in order to effectively manage threats.

4. **Timeliness of data, data accuracy, and data review.** It is important that the data received be provided to the appropriate stakeholders in a timely fashion. It is also equally important to have a data accuracy evaluation and review process. ILP will not be effective with outdated and/or inaccurate data.

5) **Institutionalising the Process.** It is essential that the tenets of ILP be consistently communicated throughout the Nigeria Police Force. Without institutionalizing the process, personnel will not fully understand the benefits of this approach and will relapse to old familiar patterns. Zonal leaders should show personnel relevant results from using ILP to inspire adoption.

6) **Zonal business process**. The Zonal Leadership team should outline the existing business processes and how ILP will be integrated into the processes. This helps to create clarity.

7) **Measuring performance.** It is vital to measure the effectiveness of any new initiative. To gauge the effectiveness of the ILP implementation, both the process and impact evaluations must be considered.

8) In today's complex environment— including constrained budgets, threats

from criminals and terrorists, and concerns about privacy and **civil** liberties—**it is important for the Police to do more with less.**

9) ILP will enable the police to **access and share comprehensive intelligence** and it helps to ensure that succinct and timely information is available to all decision makers.

10) It will provide State commands with the **capability to draw meaningful conclusions from analysed information** and make strategic, operational, and tactical decisions for effective crime reduction and threat mitigation.

11) Throughout the implementation of ILP, it is important to remember that ILP **does not change the mission of the Police**; it changes how the Police executes its mission.

Finally

Policing is increasingly relying on Intelligence to Target, Prioritise and Focus interventions. So ILP is non negotiable. It is the future of policing. The police can produce volumes of Information which only becomes useful operationally after it has been interpreted, assessed and any potential patterns and linkages investigate.

For ILP, embracing the terminology may be easier than adoption of the model itself. ILP implementation will take some time to permeate the entire policing hierarchy. It requires culture change and consistently persistent reinforcing of the message.

ILP requires a greater integration of covert information, criminal intelligence, and crime analysis to better manage risk and to support proactive policing that targets enforcement and promotes crime prevention.

YOUR NOTES ON CHAPTER FIVE

CHAPTER SIX

INTELLIGENCE-LED POLICING AND THE FUTURE OF NIGERIA POLICE FORCE

To understand why ILP has not worked and may not work in Nigeria unless drastic changes are made; we will need to look back in history. So allow me to take you back to some historical underpinnings for the way the police behave and operate in Nigeria.

Globally, policing has been going through a transition since the start of the millennium. With diverse pressures and diverging expectations, financial paucity, the concept of policing has been seeking a self-adaptive mutation for acceptance without universal success.

In a major report in 1999, Lord Patten in the UK, reflected in his submission on the review of policing in Northern Ireland by expressing the dilemmas faced by the modern police when he said:

"How can professional police officers best adapt to a world in which their own efforts are only a part of the overall policing of a modern society?...There is no perfect model for us, no example of a country that, to quote one European police officer, 'has yet finalised the total transformation from force to service'[28]

The predicament facing the police globally are being fuelled by certain key transnational developments, salient of which are:
- Transnationalism and ever increasing globalisation (Bottoms and Wiles, 1996).

---

[28] Patten Report (1999), Paragraph 1.5

- Rapid rate of Social and Technological Changes.
- Government pressure from restive citizenry dissatisfied with police status quo (Leishman, Loveday and Savage, 1995).
- Increase in non state actors aggression attacking nations from within, such as terrorism and violent militancy.
- The spread of intra-national paramilitary organisations who are challenging the settled belief of the police as the custodian of state monopoly to use force.

All these have led to a global debate on the purpose, ethics and operational parameters of the police institution. Although Lord Patten went on to declare that the purpose of the police is the protection of the human rights of the citizens; in the African and particularly Nigerian context, a slightly amended submission is required.

Despite being signatories to the Universal Declaration of Human Rights and its African version, most nations in African and Asia have slightly different posture on the universality of some rights based on their constitutional provisions.

For instance, some nations have a constitutional ban on Homosexual relationships, but some do not. Hence it is more appropriate to see policing in Nigeria and the sub-region from the prism of the need for the protection of Constitutional rights of its citizens, rather than just human rights.

So in assessing the operational effectiveness of the Nigerian police, Constitutional rights of Nigerians should be the focus of analysis and not simply the Universal Declaration of Human Rights as many tend to do.

The Nigerian constitution has many borrowed language of universal rights, but there are national peculiarities that need to be noted. For instance; the universal declaration protects the right to Family Life.

While this provision will be widely interpreted in many Western societies to include ALL manner of 'Family life'; But in the Nigerian context, same-sex couples are not recognised as "Family" as there is a prohibition against such relationships. You can now begin to see elements of national peculiarities to spectrums of these rights.

Chapter IV of the Nigerian 1999 Constitution (as amended) lists the fundamental rights of the citizens. These are similar to the European Charter of Fundamental and Human Rights, which reflects the provisions of the United Nation's Universal Declaration of Human rights.

In summary, these rights are stated in the Nigerian as follows:

    1.   Right to Life

2. Right to Respect for the dignity of a person
3. Right to Personal Liberty
4. Right to Fair Hearing
5. Right to Private and Family Life
6. Right to Freedom of thought, conscience and religion
7. Right to Freedom of expression at the Press
8. Right to Peaceful assembly and association
9. Right to Freedom of movement
10. Right to Freedom from discrimination
11. Right to Acquire and own immovable property anywhere in Nigeria

So the expectations on the Nigerian Police should be the protection of Constitutional Rights of the citizens. This allows for national particularities to be taken onto account.

To understand the sad state of the Nigerian police, a recent historical context is needful. After the military coup of 1966, the military co-opted the police into government by making two of their ranks Governors. According to Asemota,[29] the Military needed the police after the 1966 coup as the police were the only institution that had communication links all over Nigeria and had presence in every town in the country.

Hence cooperation of the police was required to sustain the military rule, especially given that at that time the army was very small in comparison to the population.

Coming out of the civil war strengthened in number and infrastructure, the military felt they no longer need the police.

So after the coup that brought General Murtala Mohammed into power, the police were no longer represented at all in government. This reality many believe was the beginning of the modern neglect of the police.

---

[29] *S.A Asemota . Policing Under Civilian and Military Administrations". in Policing*

It has been argued by some, even within the police in Nigeria that the previous military governments that ruled Nigeria for more than half of its Independent years, made deliberate efforts to emasculate and disempower the police.

This many argue was intended to ensure the police did not develop the competence, skill and capability to challenge the military through the many coups that brought the army into power.

A salient champion of this school of thought from within the police, was a police Public Relations Officer for Lagos state during the Babangida military regime in the 1980s, who was suspended and dismissed due to his "radical" claim of the disempowerment of the police by the military juntas. His name is Alozie Ogubuaja.

According to Ogubuaja:

"A military government will want a weak police force so that they can twist them as they want. The military want a weak police so that they can be used to do their biddings, the good, the bad and the ugly. Secondly, a weak and inefficient police force raises the profile of the military as masters in power. Thirdly, a strong and efficient police force is a threat to the military because there can not be two captains in one ship. The military would want a monopoly of power, to dominate and rule."[30]

While the military when in power invested and modernise themselves infrastructure wise, the police was largely under funded and neglected. But the continuing negative public perception of the role and capacity of the police is a major source of concern in a democracy.

Hence the police remain the most misunderstood profession by the general public

---

[30]<https://groups.yahoo.com/neo/groups/NIgerianWorldForum/conversations/messages/42023> accessed 22 July 2016

in Nigeria. Many expect them to work magic despite the limitations and constraints of their tools and service conditions. Their performance is weighed with misconception and ignorance, resulting in an out of context assessment of their activities.

Ignorance of the inner workings of the police and the penchant for secrecy by the Nigeria police had led to little public confidence in the service, plenty of misconception and depleted public support and cooperation with the police.

The Nigeria police are saddled with the constitutional responsibilities of prevention and detection of crime. Given the foregoing pivotal and all-encompassing roles they play, the police have become a key institution for social order in Nigeria.

Since no law operates in a vacuum, police enforcement gives value to the law and helps to regulate traditional tension between the antagonistic forces inherent in Nigerian and all human societies.

From colonial era, through military rule and the democratic dispensation, policing in Nigeria has been a tough task. Conflicts arising from social inequalities, political, religious and cultural differences appear to have widened the role and function of the police beyond the traditional law enforcement to other social services functions.

So police are working in tense environments, in which their actions or inactions do have national ramifications.

However, the Nigeria police have been under lots of public criticism, especially since the late 70s over its apparent inability to effectively prevent or control crime. Several factors have been attributed to this sorry state of affairs. Some of the key complaints are:

- Lack of professionalism, generally attributed to the recruitment policy which has on the quality of manpower.
- Poor training and institutional lack of discipline.
- Corruption and culture of bribe taking.
- Poor equipment.
- Bribe collection to work against the interest of justice. The highest bribe payers tend to get the police to support their position.

The consequence of these institutional problems is the resulting distrust and poor image and regard for the police by the citizenry.

So my key question is; Is the Nigerian Police in Transition or in Crisis? Evidence will suggest both. The scale of the change that confronts the Nigerian police suggests a crisis of immense proportion, even as it suffers from an identity crisis and transitioning to a more ethical force in an unethical criminal justice environment.

A national police force is trying to cope with a world more joined up in trade, technology and of course transnational crimes and terrorism. Its legitimacy, authority, knowledge base and competency are being challenged by these multilateral pressures. And from the evidence available, the Nigerian police appears to be an analogue force fighting in a digital age.

They are simply over their head with the challenges facing them and there appears to be no strategic review of practices and procedures as well as tools and equipment to better respond to the multiple global-scale and global-inspired challenges confronting the police in Nigeria.

Intelligence-led policing is the future of policing and the Nigeria Police Force has to adapt or be left behind.

YOUR NOTES ON CHAPTER SIX

CHAPTER SEVEN

RECOMMENDATIONS FOR IMPLEMENTING ILP IN NIGERIA

Police reform worldwide has both a technical and political angle to it. So in a federal police structure like in Nigeria, true police reform can only take place through nationwide central reform initiatives.

The changing security landscape in the past decade has placed increasing and new demands on the police globally. This realisation has created a need for revised and regular training for law enforcement personnel at all levels of command.

Law enforcement personnel have a responsibility to ensure they are up-to-date on modern day training, formal education, and become knowledgeable in tactics used by the criminal elements and how best to thwart it. Training and education is more than just sitting in a classroom and earning a certificate. It is also about applying newfound knowledge and maintaining proficiency.

Summarising the Fundamentals of Intelligence-Led Policing.

This must be led from the top, and junior officers can best deliver it. Intelligence-led policing works in tandem with community-oriented policing. It re-imagines how police can be smarter in the exercise of their unique authority and capacities by helping them more effectively decide on priorities, resource allocations and crime reduction strategies.

Intelligence-led policing is a philosophy of policing where processed information, i.e. data analysis and criminal intelligence, is pivotal to an objective, decision-making framework that facilitates crime and problem reduction, disruption and prevention through both strategic management and effective enforcement strategies that target prolific and serious offenders.

The leadership of the police are aware of the value ILP brings to the force. They have attended seminars about it from as long ago as 2011. Yet there has been no visible impact or effect of ILP within the rank and file. Even the top leadership accept they have played lip service for too long on this matter. So what is the problem?

From the preceding chapters, you have seen all the landmines along the way to implementing ILP in Nigeria. So what are my recommendations to deliver ILP to the rank and file across all zonal commands of the police?

Recommendations for implementation
My recommendations are classified into SEVEN distinct overarching groups. These are:

1.   POLICE TOP LEADERSHIP WILL.

2. GOVERNMENT AND POLITICAL WILL.
3. FUNDING
4. ENABLING INFRASTRUCTURE
5. TRAINING
6. ORGANISATIONAL AND CULTURAL CHANGE
7. INTER-AGENCY LINKAGES AND PARTNERSHIP WORKING

Police Top Leadership Will

There has to be a genuine will by the top leadership at the Force Headquarters to pursue ILP as strategy for the police operations in Nigeria. This is a first necessary and non-negotiable step.

RECOMMENDATION 1: The Inspector General of Police (IGP) and his leadership team need to produce a policy document that will commit to the implementation of ILP in Nigeria. This does not have to be detailed to start with. But a direction of travel statement must be released to all police commands stating commitment to ILP as an operation tool and technique for the force.

RECOMMENDATION 2: the IGP need to constitute an **ILP Delivery Taskforce** that will consist of internal serving officers and outside experts to come up with a detailed implementation plan.

This plan will include details of budgetary estimate, needed technical resources, phases and duration of the implementation programme as well as an Impact Assessment of ILP on the police structure and command activities and personnel.

RECOMMENDATION 3: While the Taskforce is doing their work, and after they have delivered their plan, ILP should become a permanent agenda item in all top leadership meeting the IGP has with his team.

RECOMMENDATION 4: Once the implementation plan has been produced by the

Taskforce, the IGP should constitute an **ILP DELIVERY TEAM (IDT)** to implement the plan. This team will have representation from all twelve zonal commands in the country, external experts and representative from the Federal Ministry of Justice, who will provide legal advise as needed.

RECOMMENDATION 5: Once constituted, the IGP should appoint a Deputy Inspector General of Police (DIG) that will manage the national ILP programme on a day to day basis. The IDT should report to the designated DIG.

RECOMMENDATION 6: The AIG in charge of each zone must be made to work with the IDT produce a zonal delivery plan. This plan will take account of necessary zonal variations and esoteric intelligence profiles.

It is this plan from each zone that the IDT will manage and monitor over the duration of the rollout.

Government and Political Will

The political support of the government is crucial to successfully implement ILP in Nigeria.

RECOMMENDATION 7: With many policing related agencies collecting criminal information and data as earlier explained in the book, there is a need for an Executive Order from the Presidency that will compel the sharing of intelligence and data amongst these agencies as a matter of public policy. The ideal situation will be the merger of many of these outfits with the police; but in the meantime a compulsory information sharing protocol order will be helpful to start with.

RECOMMENDATION 8: The House Committee on Police Affairs should hold bi-annual hearings to hold the IGP accountable for the implementation of ILP.

Funding

Implementing ILP will require funding. This will be a combination of funding from current or additional Federal allocation, support from the state governments, international grants and private sector contributions.

RECOMMENDATION 9: While exploring other sourcing of additional funding, the IGP must set aside some initial funding from the current police budget as well as seek state and private sector contributions for the initial phase of the implementation.

RECOMMENDATION 10: The IGP should work with the Presidency and National Assembly (if necessary); to secure specific additional funding for ILP implementation in the country.

Enabling Infrastructure

ILS need some key technical and human infrastructure to succeed. The police will need to deliver these based on the delivery plan of each zone.

RECOMMENDATION 11: To support and sustain ILP, each zone and the Force headquarters must establish a national criminal intelligence database that will contain data from all the zones and be interoperable nationwide. A criminal database is the backbone of any ILP implementation.

RECOMMENDATION 12: Each zone should allocate dedicated staffing resources for data analytics and processing at each zonal command headquarters.

RECOMMENDATION 13: Pathway need to be created in each zone for free and easy public access to report and pass data on to the police. This can be dedicated email address, text number and phone numbers.

The more information that is fed into a criminal intelligence platform, the better will be the value of the ILP that can be delivered with it.

Training.
The skill and knowledge of the police officers will determine their ability to operationalise ILP.

This must be an ongoing task throughout the implementation timeline and beyond.

RECOMMENDATION 14: A series of training programme should commence immediately ILP given the go-ahead by the IGP. Headquarters, zonal and state command staff must be trained not only in ILP principles and implementation, but also in the use of databases,

RECOMMENDATION 15: At some point a training programme on ILP should be made available to all rank and file officers on a batch basis. This training should be conducted locally in each state command.

RECOMMENDATION 16: A one-day standard ILP training programme should be developed and a roadshow should be created to deploy this training nationwide.

RECOMMENDATION 17: Zonal, state and Divisional Champions should be appointed, who will become the first point of call to local officers who have questions on ILP. These champions will be given additional training and special support to enable them act as ILP evangelist in their locality.

RECOMMENDATION 18: These Champions should then act as the user acceptance testing group for all ILP deliverables. They should receive special communications on ILP to assist their role.

Organisational and Cultural Change

The mind-set and culture of the police will need to change to allow ILP to flourish. The current culture of praising only the officers at the end of the chain who captures a criminal must end and be replaced by that which recognises all those that contributed intelligence that led to the final apprehension.

This will allow officers to think more organisational and less personal in their orientation.

RECOMMENDATION 19: The state commands should pout in place a system that will recognize the contributions of officers that are part of the chain that leads to a desirable outcome. The commands should stop focusing only on the goal scorer but on the players that supported the team and passed the ball to the scorer (so to speak)

RECOMMENDATION 20: ILP should permeate every other training programme conducted by the police. From Arrest procedure training to Interrogation techniques to custody management; officers need to be reminded always of the ILP overarching influence.

Inter-Agency Linkages and Partnership Working

There will be need to be able to obtain information from other agencies and pass on information to other agencies as well if ILP is to be established securely.

RECOMMENDATION 21: A small interoperability team should be set up by the IGP that will define and and implement a protocol on how information and intelligence will be shared with and obtained from other agencies.

Within the police, reform strategies that emphasize innovation, accountability, transparency, and professional practices should produce overall gains in efficiency, as well as greater responsiveness to the communities they serve.

There are no quick fixes to the problems facing the Nigerian Police. Improving training or salaries alone, or pressing criminal charges against selected individuals, will only produce shallow and short-term results if programs do not also correct broader institutional weaknesses that permit, enable, or encourage bad practices and unlawful conducts. International experts agree that policing reforms are long-term, even generational, efforts (Uruena, 2003; Uzendo, 2006; Neild, 2007).

ILS has the capacity to raise the standard of policing in Nigeria in a big way and the policy hierarchy should promote ILS with every vigour.

Specific details of how ILS will be delivered is the work of the Taskforce recommended in this chapter, especially as there are many ways to deliver ILS.

So this book has been a concise manual to provide the promptings and clarity needed to kick start the process of ILS implementation. I trust you have benefited from it and now determined to embrace change as the Nigerian police looks forward to the future with courage and pride.

YOUR NOTES ON CHAPTER SEVEN

OTHER BOOKS BY DR CHARLES OMOLE

RELEASED

COMING SOON

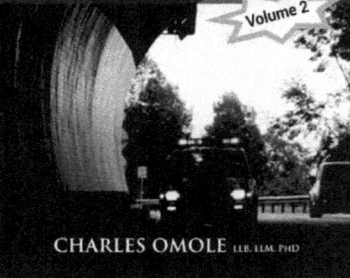

TO CONTACT DR CHARLES OMOLE:

Charlesomole@Gmail.com

Key Sections of the Police Act
(This is not a reproduction of the entire Act. Only key sections have been included to make this book a better reference guide and a one stop shop)

POLICE ACT

SECTION
1. Short title.
2. Interpretation.

ARRANGEMENT OF SECTIONS PART I
Short title and interpretation

PARTII
Constitution and employment of the force

3. Establishment of Police Force.
4. General duties of the police.
5. Constitution of the Force.
6. Command of the Force.
7. Duties of the Deputy Inspector-General of Police.
8. Duties of an Assistant Inspector-General.
9. Establishment of the Nigeria Police Council.
10. Public safety and public order.
11. Delegation by Inspector-General.
12. Command of police in case of active service.

PART III
General administration Oaths for officers

31.   Court may make orders with respect to property in possession of police.

32.   Perishable articles.

33.   The Police Reward Fund.
34.   Crying down credit.

PART Vl
Miscellaneous provisions

35.   Pay of constables not to be withheld for debt: exception.
36.   Police officers not to engage in any private business.

PART VII
Offences
37.   Offences.
38.   Apprehension of deserters.
39.   Assault on police officer.
40.   Refusing to aid police officer assaulted. 41 . Harbouring constable.
41.   Personation of police officer.
42.   Obtaining admission into Force by fraud.
43.   Ordinary course of law not to be interfered with.
44.   Persons acquitted by court not punishable on same charge under this Act, nor if convicted, except by reduction.

PART VIII
Regulations and standing orders
46.   Power to make regulations.
47.   Standing orders.

SECTION

69.   Instruction of traffic warden, etc.

CHAPTER P19
POLICE ACT
An Act to make provision for the organisation, discipline, powers and duties of the police, the special constabulary and the traffic wardens.
[1967 No. 41.]

1. Short title

[Commencement.] PART I
Short title and interpretation

[1st April, 1943]

This Act may be cited as the Police Act.
2. Interpretation
In this Act, unless the context otherwise requires-

"Commissioner" means a Commissioner of Police, a Deputy Commissioner of Po- lice or an Assistant Commissioner of Police;
"constable" means any police officer below the rank of corporal;
"court" means any court established by any law in force in Nigeria; "the Force" means the Nigeria Police Force established under this Act; "inspector" includes a chief inspector and an inspector of police;
"Inspector-General", "Deputy Inspector-General" and "Assistant Inspector- General" means respectively the Inspector-General of Police, the Deputy Inspector-General of Police and an Assistant Inspector-General of Police;

"non-commissioned officer" means a police sergeant-major, a police sergeant or a police corporal as the case may be;

"police officer" means any member of the Force;

"superintendent of police" includes a chief superintendent of police, a superintendent of police, a deputy superintendent of police, and an assistant superintendent of police;

"superior police officer" means any police officer above the rank of a cadet assistant superintendent of police;

"supernumerary police officer " means a police officer appointed under section 18, 19 or 21 of this Act or under an authorisation given under section 20 of this Act.

PART II
Constitution and employment of the Force
3. Establishment of Police Force
There shall be established for Nigeria a police force to be known as the Nigeria Police Force (in this Act referred to as "the Force").

4. General duties of the police
The police shall be employed for the prevention and detection of crime, the apprehension of offenders, the preservation of law and order, the protection of life and property and the due enforcement of all laws and regulations with which they are directly charged, and shall perform such military duties within or outside Nigeria as may be required of them by, or under the authority of this or any other Act.
[1979 No. 23.]

5. Constitution of the Force
There shall be an Inspector-General of the Nigeria Police, such number of Deputy Inspectors-General,

Assistant Inspectors-General as the Nigeria Police Council considers appropriate, a Commissioner for each State of the Federation and such ranks as may, from time to time, be appointed by the Nigeria Police Council. [1979 No. 23.]

6. Command of the Force

The Force shall be under the command of the Inspector-General, and contingents of the Force stationed in a State shall, subject to the authority of the Inspector-General, be under the command of the Commissioner of that State.

7. Duties of the Deputy Inspector-General of Police

(1)   A Deputy Inspector-General is the second in command of the Force and shall act for the Inspector-General in the Inspector-General's absence from Force Headquarters.

(2)   When acting for the Inspector-General, the Deputy Inspector-General shall be guided by the following-

(a)   all matters involving any change in Force policy shall be held in abeyance pending the return of the Inspector-General or, if the matter is urgent, referred directly to the Inspector-General for his instructions;

(b)   all matters of importance dealt with by the Deputy Inspector-General during the absence of the Inspector-General shall be referred to the Inspector-General on his return.

8. Duties of an Assistant Inspector-General

(1)   An Assistant Inspector-General shall be subordinate in rank to the Deputy Inspector-General but shall be senior to all commissioners.

(2)   An assistant Inspector-General shall act for the Inspector-General in the absence of both the Inspector-General and the Deputy Inspector-General and when so acting, the provisions of paragraphs (a) and (b) of subsection (2) of section 7 of this Act shall, with all necessary modifications, apply to him.

9. Establishment of the Nigeria Police Council

(1)   There is hereby established a body to be known as the Nigeria Police Council (in this Act referred to as "the Council") which shall consist of-

(a)   the President who shall be chairman;

(b)   the Governor of each State of the Federation;

(c)   the chairman of the Police Service Commission;

(d)   the Inspector-General of Police.

(2)   The functions of the Council shall include-

(a)   the organisation and administration of the Nigeria Police Force and all other matters relating thereto (not being matters relating to the use and operational control of the Force, or the appointment, disciplinary control and dismissal of members of the Force);

(b)   the general supervision of the Nigeria Police Force;

(c)   advising the President on the appointment of the Inspector-General of Police.

(3)   The Permanent Secretary in the Police Affairs Office, in the Presidency, shall be the Secretary to the Council and the Secretariat of the Council shall be in the Police Affairs Office, the Presidency.

[1990 No. 47.]

(4)   The President shall be charged with operational control of the Force.

(5)   The Inspector-General shall be charged with the command of the Force subject to the directive of the President.

10. Public safety and public order

(1)   The President may give to the Inspector-General such directions with respect to the maintaining and securing of public safety and public order as he may consider necessary, and the Inspector-General shall comply with those directions or cause them to be complied with.

(2)   Subject to the provisions of subsection (1) of this section, the Commissioner of a State shall comply with the directions of the Governor of the State with respect to the maintaining and securing of public safety and public order within the State, or cause them to be complied with:

Provided that before carrying out any such direction the Commissioner may request that the matter should be referred to the President for his directions.

11. Delegation by Inspector-General

The Inspector-General may, with the consent of the President by writing under his hand, delegate any of his powers under this Act (except this power of delegation) so that the delegated powers may be exercised by the delegate with respect to the matters or class of matters specified or defined in the instrument of delegation.

12. Command of police in case of active service

When required to perform military duties in accordance with the provisions of section 4 of this Act, such duties entailing service with the armed forces of Nigeria or any force for the time being attached thereto or acting therewith, the police shall be under the command and subject to the orders of the officer in command of the forces in Nigeria, but for the purposes of interior economy shall remain under the control of a superior police officer.

PART III
General administration

Oaths for officers
13. Oaths to be taken by officers on appointment
On the appointment or promotion of any person as a member of the Force to or above the rank of cadet sub-inspector, the provisions of the Oaths Act shall apply; and such per- son shall forthwith take and subscribe to the official oath, the police oath and, in proper case, the oath of allegiance.

14. Enlistment

[Cap. 01.]
Enlistment and service

Every constable, shall, on appointment, be enlisted to serve in the Force for three years, or for such other period as may be fixed by the Police Service Commission to be reckoned in all cases from the day on which he has been approved for service and taken on to the strength.

15. Extension of term of enlistment in special cases
(1)   Notwithstanding the provisions of section 14 of this Act, where a constable on or after his appointment opts or is selected for duties other than general duties and engages in those duties, he shall be deemed to have agreed to extend his period of enlistment by an additional period not exceeding six years, the extent of the

additional period to be fixed by the Police Service Commission, and the enlistment of the constable shall have effect accordingly.

(2)   Where any person to whom subsection (1) of this section applies re-engages for service with the Force, this section shall have effect in respect of the re-engagement, and notwithstanding the fact that on or after the re-engagement the person concerned is or may be a non-commissioned officer.

16. Declarations

Every non-commissioned officer, constable or recruit constable on enlistment, and every such police officer if re-engaged for a further period of service, shall make and subscribe to the police declaration prescribed by the Oaths Act.
[Cap. 01.]

17. Re-engagement

(1)   Any non-commissioned officer or constable of good character may, within six months before completion of his first period of enlistment and with the prescribed approval, re-engage to serve for a further period of six years, and may similarly re-engage for a second period of six years, and may thereafter similarly re-engage either to serve until the expiration of a third period of six years or until he reaches the age of 45 years (whichever is earlier).

(2)   Upon completion of such third period of six years, or if he has re-engaged until reaching the age of 45 years then upon reaching such age, the non-commissioned officer or constable may if he so desires and with the prescribed approval continue in the Force in the same manner in all respects as if his term of service

were still unexpired, except that he may be discharged or may claim a discharge upon six months' prescribed notice thereof being given to or by him.

(3) The prescribed approval referred to in subsections (1) and (2) of this section shall be that of the Police Service Commission or of a superior police officer to whom the Po- lice Service Commission has duly delegated the power to give such approval, and the prescribed notice referred to in subsection (2) shall be given by or to the Police Service Commission or by or to a superior police officer to whom the Police Service Commission has duly delegated the power of giving or receiving such notice.

(4) If a non-commissioned officer or constable offers to re-engage within six months after having received his discharge he will, if his offer of service is accepted, on re- engagement be entitled to the rank which he was holding at the time of his discharge, provided there is a vacancy in the establishment of that rank at the time he re-engages.

(5) The service of a non-commissioned officer or constable who has re-engaged un- der this section shall be deemed to be continuous for the purposes of the pension or annual allowance or gratuities, as the case may be, the non-commissioned officer or con- stable being regarded as being on leave without pay during the period between discharge and re-engagement.

(6) No non-commissioned officer or constable may re-engage after a period of six months has elapsed since his discharge, but a non-commissioned officer or constable may be permitted to re-enlist subsequent to that period if his offer of service is accepted.

(7) The question of the reinstatement of a re-enlisted non-commissioned officer or constable to the rank he

held prior to his discharge shall be decided by a superior police officer.

(8) Any non-commissioned officer or constable whose period of service expires during a state of war, insurrection or hostilities, may be compulsorily retained and his service prolonged for such period, not exceeding twelve months, as the Police Service Commission may direct.

(9) Subject to the provisions of section 7 (1) of the Pensions Act and to the provisions of subsection (2) of this section, no police officer other than a superior police officer shall be at liberty to resign or withdraw himself from his duties without the approval of the Police Service Commission or any police officer authorised in writing by the Police Service Commission.

[Cap. P4.]

Supernumerary police officers

18. Appointment of supernumerary police officers to protect property

(1) Any person (including any government department) who desires to avail himself of the services of one or more police officers for the protection of property owned or controlled by him may make application therefor to the Inspector-General, stating the

nature and situation of the property in question and giving such other particulars as the Inspector-General may require.

(2) On an application under the foregoing subsection the Inspector-General may, with the approval of the President, direct the appropriate authority to appoint as supernumerary police officers in the Force such number of persons as the Inspector-General thinks

requisite for the protection of the property to which the application relates.

(3)   Every supernumerary police officer appointed under this section-

(a)   shall be appointed in respect of the area of the police province or, where there is no police province, the police district or police division in which the property which he is to protect is situated;

(b)   shall be employed exclusively on duties connected with the protection of that property;

(c)   shall, in the police area in respect of which he is appointed and in any police area adjacent thereto, but not elsewhere, have the powers, privileges and immunities of a police officer; and

(d)   subject to the restrictions imposed by paragraphs (b) and (c) of this subsection and to the provisions of section 22 of this Act, shall be a member of the Force for all purposes and shall accordingly be subject to the provisions of this Act and in particular the provisions thereof relating to discipline.

(4)   Where any supernumerary police officer is appointed under this section, the per- son availing himself of the services of that officer shall pay to the **Accountant-General-**

(a)   on the enlistment of the officer, the full cost of the officer's uniform; and

(b)   quarterly in advance, a sum equal to the aggregate of the amount of the officer's pay for the quarter in question and such additional amounts as the Inspector-General may direct to be paid in respect of the maintenance of the officer during that quarter,

and any sum payable to the Accountant-General under this subsection which is not duly paid may be recovered in a summary manner before a magistrate on the complaint of any superior police officer:

Provided that this subsection shall not apply in the case of an appointment made on the application of a department of the Government of the Federation.

(5) Where the person availing himself of the services of any supernumerary police officer appointed under this section desires the services of that officer to be discontinued, he must give not less than two months' notice in writing to that effect, in the case of an officer appointed in respect of a police area within that part of Lagos State formerly known as the Federal territory, to the Inspector-General or, in the case of an officer appointed in respect of a police area within a State, to the Commissioner of Police of that State; and on the expiration of such notice the services of the supernumerary police officer in question shall be withdrawn.

(6) Where the services of a supernumerary police officer are withdrawn in pursuance of subsection (5) of this section in the course of a quarter for which the sum mentioned in subsection (4) (b) of this section has been paid to the Accountant-General, the Account- ant-General shall pay to the person by whom that sum was paid a sum which bears to that

sum the same proportion as the unexpired portion of that quarter bears to the whole of that quarter.

(6) In this section, "the Accountant-General" means the Accountant-General of the Federation; "government department" means any department of the Government of the Federation or of the Government of a State; and "quarter" means any period of three months; and any reference in this section to the person availing himself of the service of a supernumerary police officer appointed under this section is a reference to the person on whose

application the officer was appointed or, if that person has been succeeded by
some other person as the person owning or controlling the property for the protection of which the officer in question was appointed, that other person.

19. Appointment of supernumerary police officers for employment on administrative duties on police premises

(1)   The appropriate authority may, at the request of any superior police officer, appoint any person as a supernumerary police officer in the Force with a view to that per- son's employment on duties connected with the administration or maintenance of premises occupied or used for the purposes of the Force, but shall not do so in any particular case unless satisfied that it is necessary in the interests of security or discipline that per- sons performing the duties in question should be subject to the provisions of this Act relating to discipline.

(2)   Every supernumerary police officer appointed under this section-

(a)   shall be appointed in respect of the area of the police area command or where there is no police area command, the police division in which the premises in connection with whose administration or maintenance he is to be employed are situated;

(b)   shall be employed exclusively on duties connected with the administration or maintenance of those premises;

(c)   shall, in the police area in respect of which he is appointed, but not elsewhere, have the powers, privileges and immunities of a police officer; and

(d)   subject to the restrictions imposed by paragraphs (b) and (c) of this subsection and to the provisions of section 22 of this Act, shall be a member of the Force for all purposes and shall accordingly be subject to the provisions of this Act and in particular the provisions thereof relating to discipline.

20. Appointment of supernumerary police officers where necessary in the public interest

(1) If at any time the President is satisfied, as regards any police area, that it is necessary in the public interest for supernumerary police officers to be employed in that area, he may authorise the appropriate authority to appoint persons as supernumerary police officers in the Force under and in accordance with the authorisation.

(2) Every authorisation under this section shall be in writing and shall specify the police area to which it relates and the maximum number of supernumerary police officers who may be appointed under that authorisation.

(3) Every supernumerary police officer appointed under an authorisation given under this section-

(a) shall be appointed in respect of the police area to which the authorisation relates;

(b) shall, in the police area in respect of which he is appointed and in any police area adjacent thereto, but not elsewhere, have the powers, privileges and immunities of a police officer; and

(c) subject to the restriction imposed by paragraph Cb) of this subsection and to the provisions of section 22 of this Act, shall be a member of the Force for all purposes and shall accordingly be subject to the provisions of this Act and in particular to the provisions thereof relating to discipline.

21. Appointment of supernumerary police officers for attachment as orderlies

(1) The appropriate authority may at the request of the Inspector-General or of the Commissioner of Police of a State appoint any person as a supernumerary police officer in the Force with a view to that person's attachment as an orderly to-

(a)   a Minister; or

(b)   a Commissioner of the Government of a State; or

(c)   a police officer of or above the rank of assistant commissioner.

(2) Every supernumerary police officer appointed under this section-

(a)   shall be employed exclusively on duties connected with the activities of the person to whom he is attached;

(b)   shall, while so employed, have throughout Nigeria the powers, privileges and immunities of a police officer; and

(c)   subject to the restriction imposed by paragraph (a) of this subsection and to the provisions of section 22 of this Act, shall be a member of the Force for all purposes and shall accordingly be subject to the provisions of this Act and in particular the provisions thereof relating to discipline.

22. Provisions supplementary to sections 18 to 21

(1) Every supernumerary police officer shall, on appointment, be enlisted to serve in the Force from month to month, and accordingly a supernumerary police officer may at any time resign his appointment by giving one month's notice in that behalf to the superior police officer in charge of the police area in respect of which he is appointed, and his appointment may be determined by the appropriate authority on one month's

notice in that behalf or on payment of one month's pay instead of such notice.

(2) The ranks to which supernumerary police officers may be appointed shall be pre- scribed by regulations made by the President under section 46 of this Act on the recommendation of the Police Service Commission.

(3) A supernumerary police officer shall have no claim on the Police Reward Fund; and, without prejudice to any liability under the Workmen's Compensation Act, to pay compensation to or in respect of any person by virtue of his employment as a supernumerary police officer, a person's service as such as officer shall not render him or any

other person eligible for any pension, gratuity or annual allowance under this Act or the Pensions Act.

[Cap. W6. Cap. P4.]

(4) In sections 18 to 21 of this Act and this section- "the appropriate authority", in relation to any power to appoint or determine the appointment of supernumerary police officers, means the Police Service Commission or any superior police officer to whom that power has been delegated in accordance with section 216 (1) of the Constitution of the Federal Republic of Nigeria 1999;

[Cap. C23.]

"police area" means any police Area Command, police district or police division;

"Area Command", "police district" and "police di vision" means respectively an Area Command, police district or police division established under the provisions of standing orders made under section 47 of this Act.

PART IV
Powers of police officers

- 164 -

23. Conduct of prosecutions

Subject to the provisions of sections 174 and 211 of the Constitution of the Federal Republic of Nigeria 1999 (which relate to the power of the Attorney-General of the Federation and of a State to institute and undertake, take over and continue or discontinue

criminal proceedings against any person before any court of law in Nigeria), any police officer may conduct in person all prosecutions before any court, whether or not the in- formation or complaint is laid in his name.
[Cap. C23.]

24. Power to arrest without warrant

(1)   In addition to the powers of arrest without warrant conferred upon a police officer by section 10 of the Criminal Procedure Act, it shall be lawful for any police officer and any person whom he may call to his assistance, to arrest without warrant in the following cases-
[Cap. C41.]
(a)   any person whom he finds committing any felony, misdemeanour or simple offence, or whom he reasonably suspects of having committed or of being about to commit any felony, misdemeanour or breach of the peace;
(b)   any person whom any other person charges with having committed a felony or misdemeanour;
(c)   any person whom any other person-
(i)   suspects of having committed a felony or misdemeanour; or
(ii)   charges with having committed a simple offence, if such other person is willing to accompany the

police officer to the police station and to enter into a recognisance to prosecute such charge.

(2)   The provisions of this section shall not apply to any offence with respect to which it is provided that any offender may not be arrested without warrant.
(3)   For the purposes of this section the expression felony, misdemeanour and simple offence shall have the same meanings as they have in the Criminal Code.

25. Power to arrest without having warrant in possession

Any warrant lawfully issued by a court for apprehending any person charged with any offence may be executed by any police officer at any time notwithstanding that the war- rant is not in his possession at that time, but the warrant shall, on the demand of the per- son apprehended, be shown to him as soon as practicable after his arrest.

26. Summonses

Any summons lawfully issued by a court may be served by any police officer at any time during the hours of daylight.

27.   Bail of person arrested without warrant

When a person is arrested without a warrant, he shall be taken before a magistrate who has jurisdiction with respect to the offence with which he is charged or is empowered to deal with him under section 484 of the Criminal Procedure Act as soon as practicable after he is taken into custody:
[Cap. C41.J]
Provided that any police officer for the time being in charge of a police station may inquire into the case and-

(a)   except when the case appears to such officer to be of a serious nature, may release such person upon his entering into a recognisance, with or without sureties, for a reasonable amount to appear before a magistrate at the day, time and place mentioned in the recognisance; or

(b)   if it appears to such officer that such inquiry cannot be completed forthwith, may release such person on his entering into a recognisance, with or without sureties for a reasonable amount, to appear at such police station and at such times as are named in the recognisance, unless he previously receives notice in writing from the superior police officer in charge of that police station that his attendance is not required, and any such bond may be enforced as if it were a recognisance conditional for the appearance of the said person before a magistrate.

28. Power to search

(1)   A superior police officer may by authority under his hand authorise any police officer to enter any house, shop, warehouse, or other premises in search of stolen property, and search therein and seize and secure any property he may believe to have been stolen, in the same manner as he would be authorised to do if he had a search warrant, and the property seized, if any, corresponded to the property described in such search warrant.

(2)   In every case in which any property is seized in pursuance of this section, the per- son on whose premises it was at the time of seizure or the person from whom it was taken if other than the person on whose premises it was, may, unless previously charged with receiving the same knowing it to have been stolen, be summoned or arrested and brought before a magistrate to account for his possession of such property, and such magistrate shall make such order respecting the disposal of such

property and may award such costs as the justice of the case may require.

(3)   Such authority as aforesaid may only be given when the premises to be searched are, or within the preceding twelve months have been, in the occupation of any person who has been convicted of receiving stolen property or of harbouring thieves, or of any offence involving fraud or dishonesty, and punishable by imprisonment.

(4)   It shall not be necessary on giving such authority to specify any particular property, provided that the officer granting the authority has reason to believe generally that such premises are being made a receptacle for stolen goods.

29.   Power to detain and search suspected persons

A police officer may detain and search any person whom he reasonably suspects of having in his possession or conveying in any manner anything which he has reason to believe to have been stolen or otherwise unlawfully obtained.

30.   Power to take fingerprints

(1)   It shall be lawful for any police officer to take and record for the purposes of identification the measurements, photographs and fingerprint impressions of all persons who may from time to time be in lawful custody:

Provided that if such measurements, photographs and fingerprint impressions are taken of a person who has not previously been convicted of any criminal offence, and such person is discharged or acquitted by a court, all records relating to such measurements, photographs and fingerprint impressions shall be forthwith destroyed or handed over to such person.

(2)   Any person who shall refuse to submit to the taking and recording of his measurements, photographs or fingerprint impressions shall be taken before a magistrate who, on being satisfied that such person is in lawful custody, shall make such order as he thinks fit authorising a police officer to take the measurements, photographs and finger- print impressions of such person.

PART X

Special constables
49.   The Nigeria Special Constabulary
(1)   There shall continue to be a Nigeria Special Constabulary (in this Act called "the special constabulary").

(2)   The special constabulary shall be, and be deemed always to have been, part of the Nigeria Police Force, and accordingly references in this Act to the police force established under this Act shall, subject to the provisions of this Act, include, and be deemed always to have included, references to the special constabulary.

(3)   The special constabulary shall consist of-

(a)   special constables appointed in normal circumstances under section 50 of this Act; and

(b)   such emergency special constables as may be appointed from time to time un- der section 4 of this Act.

(4)   In so far as any enactment (whether passed or made before or after the commencement of this Act) requires police officers to perform military duties or confers power (whether expressly or in general terms) to require police officers to perform such duties, that enactment shall not, in the absence of express provision

to the contrary, ex- tend to members of the special constabulary.

50. Appointment of special constables in normal circumstances

(1)   Subject to the provisions of this section, the competent authority may appoint as a special constable any person (whether male or female) who-

(a)   has attained the age of21 years but has not attained the age of fifty years; and

(b)   is of good character and physically fit; and

(c)   has signified his willingness to serve as a special constable.

(2)   The President shall, from time to time, by notice published in the Federal Gazette fix the maximum number of persons who may at anyone time hold appointments under this section; and a person shall not be appointed as a special constable under this section if his appointment would cause the number for the time being so fixed to be exceeded.

(3)   Before fixing any number under subsection (2) of this section, the President shall obtain from the Nigeria Police Council a recommendation with respect thereto.

(4)   Subject to subsection (2) or this section, the Inspector-General may from time to time-

(a)   with the approval of the President fix the maximum number of persons who may at anyone time hold appointments under this section in any territory; and

(b)   at his own discretion fix the maximum number of persons appointed under this section who may at anyone time hold any particular rank in the special constabulary in any territory,

and may, in either case, fix different numbers with respect to different territories; and it shall be the duty of every competent authority to secure that the numbers fixed under this subsection are not exceeded.

(5) Every special constable appointed under this section-

(a) shall be appointed to serve as a special constable for one year or such longer period as may be agreed between him and the authority by whom he is appointed, and shall on appointment sign an engagement in the prescribed form to serve as a special constable for that period;

(b) shall be appointed in respect of the police Area Command or, where there is no police Area Command, the police division in which he resides or is employed;

(c) shall within the territory in which the police area in respect of which he is appointed is situated, but not elsewhere, have the powers, privileges and immunities of a police officer; and

(d) subject to the provisions of this Act, shall be a member of the Nigeria Police Force for all purposes:

Provided that a special constable appointed in respect of a police area within the Federal Capital Territory, Abuja shall have the powers, privileges and immunities of a police officer not only within the Federal Capital Territory, Abuja but also within any police area adjacent to the Federal Capital Territory, Abuja.

(6) A special constable appointed under this section shall have such rank as may be assigned to him by the competent authority; and where the rank of assistant superintendent or any high rank is assigned to a special constable under this subsection, the assigning authority shall cause notice thereof to be published in the Federal Gazette.

(7) A special constable appointed under this section may within three months before the end of his first or any subsequent period of engagement, and with the

permission of the competent authority, re-engage to serve for a further period of one year or such longer period as may be agreed between him and that authority and, if he does so, his appointment under this section shall be deemed to have been extended accordingly; and without prejudice to the right of the competent authority to refuse permission in any case, a per- son shall not be permitted to re-engage under this subsection unless he would, if not al- ready a special constable, be qualified for appointment as such under subsection (1) above.

(8)   Every special constable appointed under this section shall, on appointment, be is- sued with a certificate of appointment in the prescribed form, and on the determination of his appointment (whether by the passage of time or under section 51 of this Act) shall be issued with a certificate of discharge in the prescribed form.

(9)   In relation to constables appointed under this section-

(a)   section 16 hereof (which relates to the making of a declaration on enlistment or re-engagement) shall have effect as if for the reference to enlistment there were substituted a reference to appointment; and

(b)   section 17 of this Act (which relates to re-engagement) shall not apply.

51. Resignation, sus pension and dis missal of constables appointed under section 50

(1)   A special constable appointed under section 50 of this Act may at any time give to the superior police officer in charge of the police area in respect of which he is appointed notice in writing to the effect that he desires to resign his appointment on a date (not being less than fourteen days later than the date on which the notice is given) mentioned in the notice.

(2)   On receipt of a notice under the foregoing subsection the superior police officer in question shall refer it to the competent authority; and if, but only if, the competent authority consents to the notice having effect, the appointment of the special constable by whom the notice was given shall determine on the date mentioned in the notice or the date on which he is notified that the competent authority has given his consent under this subsection, whichever is the later.

(3)   The competent authority may at any time, for reasons appearing to him to be sufficient, by notice in writing forthwith suspend or determine the appointment of any special constable appointed under section 50 of this Act and may, if he thinks fit, do so with- out informing the special constable of the reasons for his action, but shall in every case immediately report his action and the reasons therefor to the Inspector-General.

(4)   A special constable whose appointment is suspended or determined under sub- section (3) of this section otherwise than by the Nigeria Police Council, may appeal

against the suspension or determination to the competent authority; and any such appeal shall be heard and determined by the competent authority to whom it is made.

(5)   Any delegation of the powers of the Nigeria Police Council under subsections (3) and (4) of this section shall be such as to secure that in every case the competent authority

having power to hear and determine an appeal under subsection (4) of this section is a police officer of higher rank than the police officer against whose action the appeal is brought.

52. Appointment of emergency special constables

(1)   If at any time the Commissioner of Police for a State is satisfied, as regards any police area in that State, that an unlawful assembly or riot or breach of the peace has taken place or may reasonably be expected to take place in that area, or that by reason of other special circumstances it is necessary in the public interest for emergency special constables to be appointed in respect of that area, he may authorise the superior police officer in charge of that area or any chief superintendent of police to appoint persons resident or employed in that area (whether male or female) as emergency special constables.

(2)   An authorisation under this section need not be in writing, but must specify the maximum number of emergency special constables who may be appointed under that authorisation.

(3)   Where a superior police officer proposes to appoint any person as an emergency special constable under an authorisation given under this section, he shall cause to be
served on that person a notice in the prescribed form requiring him to present himself at a time and place specified in the notice for appointment as an emergency special constable.

(4)   Every person on whom a notice is served under subsection (3) of this section shall present himself at the time and place specified in the notice and shall there, on being required to do so by the superior police officer proposing to appoint him, make and sign a promise in the prescribed form to serve as an emergency special constable until such time as his appointment is determined under this section; and immediately after he has made and signed that promise, the superior police

officer shall hand to him a document in the prescribed form appointing him as an emergency special constable in respect of the police area to which the authorisation under which he is being appointed relates.

(5)   Every emergency special constable appointed under this section-

(a)   shall, in the police area in respect of which he is appointed, but not elsewhere, have the powers, privileges and immunities of a police officer; and

(b)   subject to the provisions of this Act, shall be a member of the Nigeria Police Force for all purposes and shall accordingly be subject to the provisions of this Act.

(6)   The superior police officer in charge of the police area in respect of which an emergency special constable is appointed may at any time, and shall if so directed by the Commissioner of Police for the State in which that police area is situated, by notice in writing forthwith, or with effect from a future date specified in the notice, determine the emergency special constable's appointment; and on the determination of his appointment under this section an emergency special constable shall be issued with a certificate of discharge in the prescribed form.

(7)   Any person who without reasonable excuse (proof of which shall lie on him)-

(a)   refuses or fails to comply with the requirements of a notice served on him un- der subsection (3) of this section; or

(b)   refuses to make and sign a promise to serve on being required to do so under subsection (4) of this section,

shall be liable on summary conviction to a fine not exceeding forty naira.

(8)   The foregoing provisions of this section shall apply in relation to the Federal Capital Territory, Abuja

as they apply in relation to a State, subject to the modification that, in relation to the Federal Capital Territory, Abuja any reference to the Commissioner of Police shall be construed as a reference to the Inspector-General of Police.

(9)   The foregoing provisions of this section shall have effect subject to section 53 (2) and (3) of this Act.

www.ingramcontent.com/pod-product-compliance
Lightning Source LLC
Chambersburg PA
CBHW060028210326
41520CB00009B/1037